Understanding the Bible today

Old Testament

Prophets

Eight Bible studies for student and young adult groups

by Tom Stuckey

Jigsaw Series

Series editor: Jim Belben

Bible Society

BIBLE SOCIETY
Stonehill Green, Westlea, Swindon SN5 7DG, England.

First published 1985

British Library Cataloguing in Publication Data
Stuckey, Tom
Old Testament Prophets: eight Bible studies for student and young adult groups – (Understanding the Bible today) – (Jigsaw series).
1. Bible. O.T. Prophets – Commentaries
I. Title II. Bible. O.T. Prophets. *English. Selections. 1985* III. Series.
224′.06 BS1286
ISBN 0-564-07462-4

Printed in Great Britain by
Stanley L. Hunt (Printers) Ltd, Midland Road, Rushden, Northants.

Bible Societies exist to provide resources for Bible distribution and use. Bible Society in England and Wales (BFBS) is a member of the United Bible Societies, an international partnership working in over 150 countries. Their common aim is to reach all people with the Bible, or some part of it, in a language they can understand and at a price they can afford. Parts of the Bible have now been translated into approximately 1,800 languages. Bible Societies aim to help every church at every point where it uses the Bible. You are invited to share in this work by your prayers and gifts. Bible Society in your country will be very happy to provide details of its activity.

CONTENTS

Foreword

I heard of a recent Bible study in which the members came to blows! They were not, I hasten to add, using this book at the time. But if, like them, your group finds it difficult to handle differing Christian view points on the many social, economic, and political issues that make up life in society, you may not yet be ready for this book. It is a guide to the Old Testament prophets, but it aims to get a group thoroughly involved with the prophets' passionate protest for God and his justice. It plants us firmly in the prophets' shoes.

The historical background to the prophets' ministry is given in helpful notes, but the guide moves beyond cold facts. Dramas and role-plays make us aware of the feelings the prophets had as they shared God's word.

Still, the process does not end there. It is not enough to take a journey back in time to the issues of the past. There are real issues today which are an affront to the goodness of God. What are they? How would the prophets address them? This guide helps the group to face these questions together with honesty and with feeling.

There will be many of us for whom the radical protests of the prophets strike a deep chord. Others, no doubt, will plead caution and realism. Both need honestly to share with each other. Both need to be open to the naked simplicity of the prophets' concern that God's will for justice be done. And if there are differences of opinion, we do well to remember that prophecy does not stand alone in the Scriptures. It is balanced by the wisdom of Proverbs whose writers bolster society even while the prophets are calling for radical change.

Applying the prophets' message could require one more major leap in our thinking. In the West people tend to argue that if each individual was obedient to God then as a result we would have a better community life.

The opposite is true in many other cultures. The Old Testament prophets, in particular, expressed their faith as it related to the life of the community. They addressed a community as a whole with God's demands as to how that community should live. Within that community framework each individual was to work out his or her own obedience.

If we are to get to grips with the Old Testament prophets then we must allow ourselves to hear the prophets as prophets to a community, speaking about the community's life *together.*

This is what Tom Stuckey's volume helps us to do. This way of looking at things may be new and, for some, controversial. But it will certainly prove an invigorating stimulus to those who feel they already have many of the answers or who feel there are no more questions.

Things start to happen when God's people meet round his word. Tom Stuckey's guide should certainly help get things going.

Christopher Sugden
Registrar of the Oxford Centre for Mission Studies

Introduction

The diversity of the Bible

Many pieces . . .

The Bible is a vast library. Letters, poems and biography stand side-by-side with prayers, proverbs and family trees. To confuse matters further, a single book, and sometimes a single passage, can contain many different styles. Finding your way about can be a very difficult business. So it is no surprise that many readers steer clear of all but the most popular books.

First and foremost, this series aims to set out a simple method for helping you understand any material you find in the Bible; to help you explore the unfamiliar books; to help you understand and apply what you find.

All the Bible is relevant. Although not all passages are directly applicable to you now, all were directly relevant to someone at some time. Discovering what God was saying to the original hearers is one key to understanding what God, through the Holy Spirit, is saying to you now.

Through this series you can discover an original approach to reading law, history, poetry and prophets in the Old Testament; gospels and letters in the New Testament. You can refer back to this method in years to come – and use this as a valuable reference book.

. . . One picture

One factor holds all the diverse contents of the Bible together – it is about how God reveals himself to ordinary people. Although it is written by human writers, God's Spirit initiates and controls. God still speaks to us through its pages – thus we can refer to it as the "Word of God".

Of course, a method is not enough on its own. Many questions will be raised which cannot be answered simply. You will need to explore further on your own. But this method can help you cope with obscure material. Whether you are used to studying the Bible or not, this book will, I hope, open up new ideas and possibilities. It can help you think in the broadest terms – "What is God saying to me in this passage?"

The prophets

A prophet is a person who receives and passes on a message from God, so it is no surprise that the Bible is full of them! Over half of the Old Testament and some of the New contains prophetic material, because even the so-called "historical books" have, as we will see, a prophetic slant. I do not intend, however, to explore "prophecy" in general. This book concentrates on those Old Testament characters, Isaiah through to Malachi, whose sayings cover about one quarter of the Old Testament. Of those, we will concentrate particularly on Isaiah, Jeremiah and Ezekiel – the so-called "major" prophets. You might be surprised to find no mention of the important prophetic figures, Moses and Elijah, who were the models for all the prophets of Israel, but they will be dealt with in another volume on Old Testament history. Similarly, "apocalyptic" literature such as Daniel and Revelation is not covered in this volume.

The eight sessions of this book are split into two units. Unit 1 looks at the prophets in their context. How were the prophets influenced by past tradition? How did they receive their message? How did they view the society in which they lived? What were their visions of the future? All these factors shaped their message. To understand their message it is essential to understand this context.

Unit 2 then seeks to understand and apply the prophet's message. We will see the effect of the message on the prophet himself. We will see the prophets as spiritual and political giants yet as fragile human beings. We will seek to learn from their creative methods as well as learning from their message.

If this book succeeds, then its methods will quickly become second nature to you. To begin with, I have had to move slowly through questions that later you will be able to use instinctively.

Throughout both units, however, my ultimate aim is to encourage you as a group to engage in prophetic activity. The apostle Paul speaks of prophecy as one of the gifts of the Holy Spirit to his church. Of course, our responses will appear weak and insignificant when compared with the activity of the great Old Testament figures, yet we shall at least attempt to make a start. The Holy Spirit can speak through prophets in every day and age, including our own. The torch first lit by those men and women of the Old Testament is still being carried today and may well be passed over to you.

In the days of the Old Testament when the division of sacred and secular was not as clear as it is now, the prophets spoke to society as a whole and not just to a religious sector. This is a role we sadly neglect today. This volume attempts to redress the balance – to see how the prophet can speak to society rather than to the Church. Some members of the group may feel a measure of frustration with this approach – they may want to look at topics that are more church-centred and less political.

I would encourage you, however, to either stay with this book to discover the rewards of this approach, or to look at another volume of the *Jigsaw* series which looks at a more central concern of the members.

How to use this book

The most important features of this book are the eight *Steps for understanding prophecy* which are introduced session by session (and are also gathered for easy reference on the inside back flap). They are not in any strict order, and there is obviously some overlap between the sessions, but using these steps you should eventually be able to make sense of most Old Testament prophets. The step-by-step approach means that you must tackle the sessions in the order they appear, because each session assumes some familiarity with the previous ones.

I assume you will be doing one session per week. The maximum benefit will be obtained by doing all eight sessions over an eight-week stretch – but if that is impossible the two units can be approached in two four-week stretches.

The sessions are designed to be easy to lead – and to let everyone participate. You don't need to have any prior knowledge of the passages you are studying – though it will always help if you have read them through beforehand.

As well as getting to know the Bible, through these studies you will be able to get to know the rest of the group better, to learn from your shared experiences, and to apply to your own life what the Holy Spirit teaches you, through the Bible.

This is a members', rather than a leaders' book, so everyone in the group will need a copy of this volume. It includes all the passages that you will be studying as well as essential background material, to give you a wide perspective of the prophets.

Each session has three parts:

Bible study

– introduces a *Step for understanding prophecy*
– gets you applying it to a relevant text
– provides historical and cultural background where necessary.
– Allow 30 minutes for this part.

Application

– draws on your contemporary experience
– encourages you to look prophetically at society around you.
– Allow anything from 30 minutes to 1 hour for this part.

On your own

– suggests other material for anyone who wants to apply the methods of the session to another prophet.

Getting the most out of these Bible studies

★ A good size for a group is from 5 to 11 people.

★ The time needed for a session will vary between 1 and 1½ hours, with coffee either at the beginning or at the end. Begin with a prayer. Sometimes you may also wish to sing. Decide at your first meeting what each session should consist of, then who should lead each week. Arrange things so that adequate time is available for each activity.

★ Always try to start on time.

★ Bring your own copy of this book and a pencil and rubber to each session. Keep a record or summary of your own opinions and discoveries to refer to at later sessions.

★ A lot of use is made of sub-groups of three or four people. It helps everyone to have their say! When such groups are suggested, remain more or less sitting where you are and simply chat to your immediate neighbours for a minute or so, but try not to seek out the same few people every time.

"Thank you for such a good turnout this week!"

How to lead these Bible studies

★ It might help if the group has the same leader for the first three sessions. Afterwards the leadership should rotate.

★ Activities within each session are designed to encourage movement, interest, and maximum participation. They are simply *suggestions to help* the group function effectively rather than laws to be followed slavishly, but where, for example, role-play or drama is suggested, don't pass over it with the comment, "It's not for our group." I think you will find it good fun, and that it adds an extra dimension to your exploration. Dotted throughout the sessions are discussion questions, marked . Use these to aid discussion if necessary.

★ It can be helpful to make a contract or promise with regard to this course, to attend regularly, and to participate fully. The promise is simply made to the rest of the group, in order that everyone might feel more committed. If you wish to use this contract, then I suggest the promise is discussed and agreed to at the end of the first session, and then renewed at the fourth session.

Preparing

★ Read the introductory material (everything before session 1) so that you are completely familiar with the assumptions and limitations of this book. Be ready to remind members of these assumptions if necessary.

★ Read through the sessions you are to lead. Estimate how much time needs to be spent on the various activities of: 1. Bible study and 2. Application. The clocks in the margin indicate suggested timings. Make sure that the group makes the best use of time by *starting* the session on time and *keeping* to the pace you have set so that all appropriate material is covered.

★ Have plenty of plain paper and pens for each session. Also have large sheets of paper (wallpaper or newsprint will do) and felt-tipped pens, to help summarize group discussion.

★ Where role-play and drama is required, ensure that there is space available (even two rooms where the group can work separately). Props may also be needed. In a further session we will spend time meditating. Ensure that the room is quiet.

At the session

★ Be ready well before the starting time. Make sure that the room is adequately set up and arrangements are made for having a drink of coffee.

★ Unless there seems a good reason not to, the aims and background, as well as the Bible passages, should be read out loud in the group. Give it a few moments to sink in, then ask a simple question such as, "Any reactions?" or "Do you agree?" etc., before going on to the specific task. Likewise, after examining the diagram simply ask, "Do you agree?" or "Any comments?"

★ When any passage is first read it makes certain obvious connections with a person's life – it is good group practice to allow the group members to express and discuss "connections" for a short while before applying the method to it. As above, ask a simple question such as, "Any reactions?" or "What strikes you most in that passage?"

★ When sub-groups are feeding back to the whole group it can get quite repetitive, or else the latter groups simply say "we thought the same". So make sure the same group does not feed back first every time.

★ During discussion and when necessary, get someone to write up the group findings on a large sheet of paper.

★ Recognize "red herrings" and keep the group to its central task. Remember, however, that you are not a dictator, and you must not talk all the time. You are there to help everyone join in. Encourage quiet people. Quieten talkative people.

★ At the end, make sure that next week's leader is appointed and that the group know of anything they need for the next session. You might wish to suggest that group members read next week's passages.

1 What is a Prophet?

Aim

To get to know other members of the group better and to look at a prophet in the Old Testament.

Bible study

★ Begin with this activity, even if you are a well-established group. It introduces the theme of the session and it's amazing what you may find out!

Get together in pairs. Make sure you are with a person you don't know very well. Try to find out all you can about each other. (i.e. Where do you live? What family have you got? What do you like doing? etc.)

Reassemble and take it in turns to introduce your partner to the rest of the group.

★ Seeing the prophets in context means first of all seeing them as real people, speaking to real audiences. Read the following account of one of the early prophets, and the background material which follows it.

Deborah and Barak

4 After Ehud died, the people of Israel
sinned against the LORD again. 2 So
the LORD let them be conquered by Jabin,
a Canaanite king who ruled in the city
of Hazor. The commander of his army
was Sisera, who lived at Harosheth-of-the-
Gentiles. 3 Jabin had nine hundred iron
chariots, and he ruled the people of Israel
with cruelty and violence for twenty
years. Then the people of Israel cried out
to the LORD for help.
4 Now Deborah, the wife of Lappidoth,
was a prophet, and she was serving as
a judge for the Israelites at that time.
5 She used to sit under a certain palm-tree
between Ramah and Bethel in the hill-
country of Ephraim, and the people of
Israel would go there for her decisions.
6 One day she sent for Barak son of
Abinoam from the city of Kedesh in
Naphtali and said to him, "The LORD, the
God of Israel, has given you this
command: 'Take ten thousand men from
the tribes of Naphtali and Zebulun and
lead them to Mount Tabor. 7 I will bring
Sisera, the commander of Jabin's army,
to fight against you at the River Kishon.
He will have his chariots and soldiers,
but I will give you victory over him.' "
8 Then Barak replied, "I will go if you
go with me, but if you don't go with me,
I won't go either."
9 She answered, "All right, I will go
with you, but you won't get any credit
for the victory, because the LORD will hand
Sisera over to a woman." So Deborah set
off for Kedesh with Barak. 10 Barak called
the tribes of Zebulun and Naphtali to
Kedesh, and ten thousand men followed
him. Deborah went with him.

11 In the meantime Heber the Kenite
had set up his tent close to Kedesh near
the oak-tree at Zanannim. He had moved
away from the other Kenites, the descendants of Hobab, the brother-in-law of
Moses.
12 When Sisera learnt that Barak had
gone up to Mount Tabor, 13 he called out
his nine hundred iron chariots and all his
men, and sent them from Harosheth-of-
the-Gentiles to the River Kishon.
14 Then Deborah said to Barak, "Go!
The LORD is leading you! Today he has
given you victory over Sisera." So Barak
went down from Mount Tabor with his
ten thousand men. 15 When Barak attacked with his army, the LORD threw
Sisera into confusion together with all his
chariots and men. Sisera got down from
his chariot and fled on foot. 16 Barak
pursued the chariots and the army to
Harosheth-of-the-Gentiles, and Sisera's
whole army was killed. Not a man was
left.

(Judges 4.1-16)

Background

Bethel was one of the ancient holy places associated with Jacob, the "father of Israel". In those early times (twelfth century BC) the leaders of the clans or tribes of Israel were called judges because they were responsible for dispensing justice and arbitrating in disputes. They included both men and women. They retained their position as leaders only as long as they were effective in both peace and war. This effectiveness was dependent on a personal charisma which was seen as the power of the Spirit of the Lord upon them.

Ehud, one of the judges before Deborah, had driven the Moabite enemy across the Jordan and secured peace for Israel for over 50 years. They now faced a new foe (possibly the Philistines) who had advanced from the north, across the Esdraelon plain.

★ This prophecy was uttered more than 3,000 years ago. Can it possibly be relevant to us today? How can we learn from it?

Every prophecy has a chain of audiences. This is no exception! God speaks to Deborah; who then speaks to Barak; who then, as army commander, presumably addresses the soldiers of Zebulun and Naphtali. People who remember the story then retell it to audiences of later generations, one of which eventually writes it down. Further audiences read this prophecy over the centuries until the message reaches us today. We shall explore aspects of this chain in later sessions.

One way of approaching a prophecy is to begin at the beginning of this chain and relate to the situation/character of the prophet through whom God spoke, and the audiences he spoke to. So:

Find out all you can about the prophet and the audience

★ Break up into two sub-groups to examine the passage and background material. One sub-group attempt to find out all it can about Deborah and the other about the audience, which in this case was initially Barak, the army commander.

Headings like these may help you gather appropriate information:
- name(s)?
- family?
- location?
- status?
- what he/she says and does?
- how does your character view the others?

Try to think yourself into the attitudes of Deborah and Barak. Prepare a character outline, which helps to describe them. Get someone in each sub-group to write out the character outline.

★ Reassemble. Read back the character outlines and discuss:

What kind of people were Deborah and Barak?
To whom would you compare them today?

As this discussion happens, set out below your own summary.

Character outline of Deborah	Character outline of Barak

Background

The outcome was evidently very successful for Deborah and Barak. Reading between the lines it seems that there was a sudden thunderstorm and the chariot wheels became stuck in the mud. Deborah expressed her joy in:

The Song of Deborah and Barak

5 On that day Deborah and Barak son of Abinoam sang this song:

2 Praise the LORD!
The Israelites were determined to fight;
the people gladly volunteered.
3 Listen, you kings!
Pay attention, you rulers!
I will sing, I will play music
to Israel's God, the LORD.

4 LORD, when you left the mountains of Seir,
when you came out of the region of Edom,
the earth shook, and rain fell from the sky.
Yes, water poured down from the clouds.

5 The mountains quaked before the LORD of Sinai,
before the LORD, the God of Israel.

(Judges 5.1-5)

★ Even with long passages it is often useful to attempt to summarize the prophet's message, particularly looking for any summary statements in the passage. For the next five minutes, in the same pairs as at the beginning, look again at all the passages above and briefly summarize below what you understand Deborah's message to be.

Message

....

....

....

....

....

....

....

....

★ Share this with the whole group, and discuss the differences between them.

Which one best expresses what you think God wanted to say?

★ Over the course of this book we will build up a diagram which will summarize this method of looking at prophets. Step 1 is summarized in diagram 1 below.

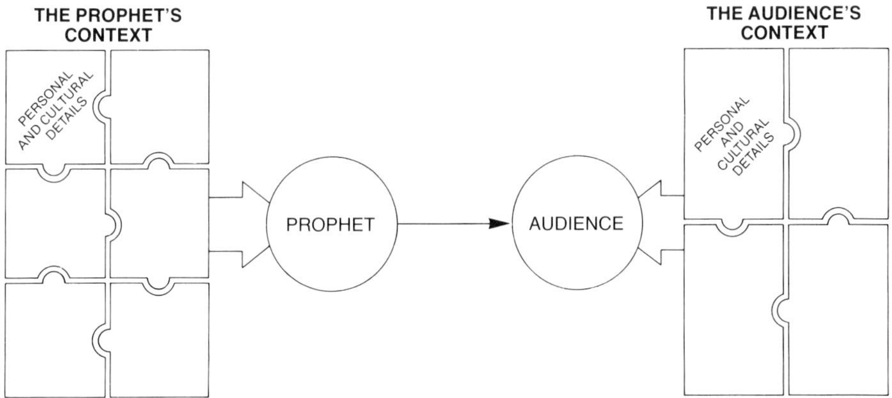

Diagram 1

Application

★ The title of this session is, What is a prophet? In the light of the discussions so far, what is your definition of a prophet? On your own, write it below. Only take a couple of minutes. This is a working definition – there will be a chance to review it in later sessions.

A prophet is . . . .

. . . .

. . . .

. . . .

. . . .

★ Who, if anyone, do you think of as "today's prophets", and why? Discuss this briefly with your next-door-neighbour. Let each pair nominate a possible candidate, giving reasons for the choice and outlining something about their candidate's message and character. Discuss the various nominations, trying to decide which ones are appropriate.

★ As a group, discuss what the main thing is that each of you has learnt from this session.

★ Finally, if you are going to use the group "promise" or contract (see page 11) discuss it now.

On your own

A similar story is found in 1 Samuel 3.1-18. Further information about Samuel and Eli is found in 1 Samuel 1.9-22 and 2.12-17.

Summary of the first step

Find out all you can about the prophet and the audience

2 Called by God

Aim
To see how the experience of being called by God gave a prophet a unique perspective from which to view the world.

Bible study

★ Seeing the prophets in context means seeing them as people called by God, with a message to pass on.

Again and again we read in the stories of the prophets, "I heard the LORD say . . " The mark of a prophet, then as now, is the ability to hear what God is saying, and to pass it on faithfully. This was the significance of their divine calling. So:

Explore the prophet's calling

This perspective is set out in diagram 2 below.

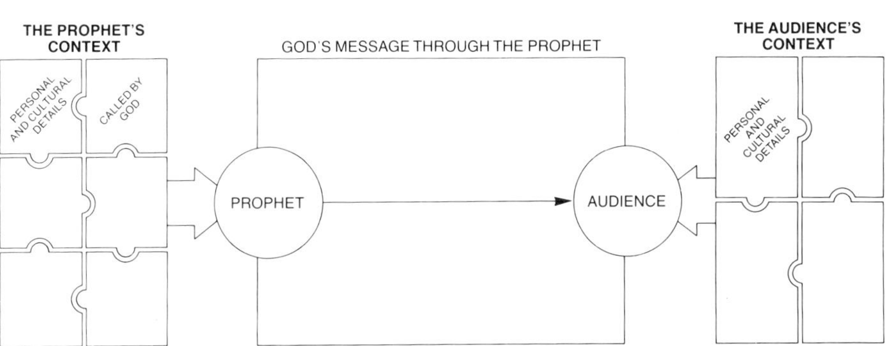

Diagram 2

★ In two sub-groups, read one of the two passages below, which describe the calls of Isaiah and Jeremiah. Their experiences were very different, yet as they came into direct contact with God, both were given a unique ability to see, hear, and speak in a new way. Read your passages and the background material. Then consider the following questions, aiming to think yourselves imaginatively into the experience of the prophet:

- **What was he feeling?**
- **What actually happened? – speculate if necessary.**
- **What do you think God was giving to him?**

◔ Then, finally, share your main findings with the rest of the group.

God Calls Isaiah to Be a Prophet

6 In the year that King Uzziah died,
I saw the Lord. He was sitting on
his throne, high and exalted, and his robe
filled the whole Temple. 2 Round him
flaming creatures were standing, each of
which had six wings. Each creature
covered its face with two wings, and its
body with two, and used the other two
for flying. 3 They were calling out to each
other:

"Holy, holy, holy!
The LORD Almighty is holy!
His glory fills the world."

4 The sound of their voices made the
foundation of the Temple shake, and the
Temple itself was filled with smoke.
5 I said, "There is no hope for me! I
am doomed because every word that
passes my lips is sinful, and I live among
a people whose every word is sinful. And
yet, with my own eyes, I have seen the
King, the LORD Almighty!"
6 Then one of the creatures flew down
to me, carrying a burning coal that he
had taken from the altar with a pair of
tongs. 7 He touched my lips with the
burning coal and said, "This has touched
your lips, and now your guilt is gone, and
your sins are forgiven."
8 Then I heard the Lord say, "Whom
shall I send? Who will be our messenger?"
I answered, "I will go! Send me!"
9 So he told me to go and give the people
this message: "No matter how much you
listen, you will not understand. No matter
how much you look, you will not know
what is happening."

(Isaiah 6.1-9)

Jeremiah

1 This book is the account of what was
said by Jeremiah son of Hilkiah, one
of the priests of the town of Anathoth
in the territory of Benjamin. 2 The LORD
spoke to Jeremiah in the thirteenth year
that Josiah son of Amon was king of
Judah, 3 and he spoke to him again when
Josiah's son Jehoiakim was king. After
that, the LORD spoke to him many times,
until the eleventh year of the reign of
Zedekiah son of Josiah. In the fifth month
of that year the people of Jerusalem were
taken into exile.

The Call of Jeremiah

4 The LORD said to me, 5 "I chose you
before I gave you life, and before you
were born I selected you to be a prophet
to the nations."
6 I answered, "Sovereign LORD, I don't
know how to speak; I am too young."

7 But the LORD said to me, "Do not say
that you are too young, but go to the
people I send you to, and tell them
everything I command you to say. 8 Do
not be afraid of them, for I will be with
you to protect you. I, the LORD, have
spoken!"
9 Then the LORD stretched out his hand,
touched my lips, and said to me, "Listen,
I am giving you the words you must speak.
10 Today I give you authority over nations
and kingdoms to uproot and to pull down,
to destroy and to overthrow, to build and
to plant."

(Jeremiah 1.1–9)

9 But when I say, "I will forget the LORD
and no longer speak in his name,"
then your message is like a fire
burning deep within me.
I try my best to hold it in,
but can no longer keep it back.

(Jeremiah 20.9)

Background

Isaiah lived in Jerusalem in the latter half of the eighth century, whilst Jeremiah lived there about one hundred years later. During that time Jerusalem miraculously survived. The Assyrian armies who stood posed and ready to strike were suddenly withdrawn. An overthrow of government at home and the emergence of Babylon as the new world power gave Jerusalem a breathing space. At the end of the seventh century that time had been used up. Assyria was finished as a world power, but the forces of Babylon were marching slowly but relentlessly on. Jeremiah lived and worked under the shadow of this more ominous opponent. (See time chart on back flap.)

★ To help summarize these two passages, spend 10 minutes as a group considering the following question:

From the evidence of these two stories, what would you say were the essential qualifications of an Old Testament prophet?

It might help if you actually draw up a "job description", indicating essential qualifications, previous experience, etc.

★ Of course, not all calls are as spectacular as those of Isaiah and Jeremiah. Read the following passages which describe the experiences of Habakkuk and Amos, then discuss:

What is the key image or picture in each passage?
What is distinctive about this prophet's calling?

The LORD's Answer to Habakkuk

2 I will climb my watch-tower and wait
to see what the LORD will tell me
to say and what answer he will give to
my complaint.
2 The LORD gave me this answer:
"Write down clearly on clay tablets what
I reveal to you, so that it can be read
at a glance. 3 Put it in writing, because
it is not yet time for it to come true.
But the time is coming quickly, and what
I show you will come true. It may seem
slow in coming, but wait for it; it will
certainly take place, and it will not be
delayed. 4 And this is the message: 'Those
who are evil will not survive, but those
who are righteous will live because they
are faithful to God.' "

(Habakkuk 2.1-4)

A Vision of a Plumb-Line

7 I had another vision from the Lord.
In it I saw him standing beside a wall
that had been built with the help of a
plumb-line, and there was a plumb-line
in his hand. 8 He asked me, "Amos, what
do you see?"
"A plumb-line," I answered.
Then he said, "I am using it to show
that my people are like a wall that is
out of line. I will not change my mind
again about punishing them. 9 The places
where Isaac's descendants worship will
be destroyed. The holy places of Israel
will be left in ruins. I will bring the dynasty
of King Jeroboam to an end."

(Amos 7.7-9)

Application

★ God calls in many ways. After thinking on your own for a few minutes, tell a partner about any occasion when you felt called by God.

What particular insight or emphasis did God give you on that occasion?

Briefly share this with the rest of the group and discuss:

How can we better prepare ourselves to hear God's call?

On your own

Another more complex portrayal of a prophet's calling is found in Ezekiel, chapters 1 and 2.

Summary of the second step

Explore the prophet's calling

3 The present situation

Aim

To examine how a prophet saw his society, and how he responded to it.

Bible study

★ Seeing the prophets in context means seeing them within their own society with all its problems. This session looks at Amos and his struggles with the Israelite people.

The story and message of many of the early prophets like Samuel, Deborah and Elijah has to be extracted from the books of so-called Old Testament history. As time passed, however, there was a growing interest not so much in the story, but in the message of the prophet. The speeches, sayings, sermons and oracles of particular prophets were gathered to form separate books. Amos, who lived in the eighth century, was one of the first prophets to have his message recorded at length under his own name.

★ Read through the following passages, which provide an introduction to Amos.

---

1 These are the words of Amos, a
shepherd from the town of Tekoa.
Two years before the earthquake, when
Uzziah was king of Judah and Jeroboam
son of Jehoash was king of Israel, God
revealed to Amos all these things about
Israel.
2 Amos said,

"The Lord roars from Mount Zion;
his voice thunders from Jerusalem.
The pastures dry up,
and the grass on Mount Carmel turns
brown."

(Amos 1.1-2)

Amos and Amaziah

10 Amaziah, the priest of Bethel, then
sent a report to King Jeroboam of Israel:
"Amos is plotting against you among the
people. His speeches will destroy the
country. 11 This is what he says: 'Jeroboam will die in battle, and the people
of Israel will be taken away from their
land into exile.' "
12 Amaziah then said to Amos, "That's
enough, prophet! Go on back to Judah
and do your preaching there. Let *them*
pay you for it. 13 Don't prophesy here at
Bethel any more. This is the king's place of
worship, the national temple."
14 Amos answered, "I am not the kind
of prophet who prophesies for pay. I am
a herdsman, and I take care of fig-trees.
15 But the Lord took me from my work
as a shepherd and ordered me to come
and prophesy to his people Israel. 16 So
now listen to what the Lord says. You
tell me to stop prophesying, to stop raving
against the people of Israel. 17 And so,
Amaziah, the Lord says to you, 'Your wife
will become a prostitute on the streets,
and your children will be killed in war.
Your land will be divided up and given
to others, and you yourself will die in
a heathen country. And the people of
Israel will certainly be taken away from
their own land into exile.' "

(Amos 7.10-17)

★ Get together in two groups and write below all the information revealed by these passages about the character of either Amos or Amaziah.

Character of Amos	Character of Amaziah

★ Now share and discuss your findings and the following questions:

Could Amos or Amaziah have become a leader in your church?

What was the relationship between Amos and Amaziah?

★ Read the background below. Does this cast any new light upon your discoveries?

Background

During the 400 years between Deborah and Amos, two very important historical changes had taken place. First, the judges, or prophets, were no longer the military and national leaders. Israel (during the time of the prophet Samuel) had appointed its own king, a man called Saul, and tension arose inevitably as each sought to exercise leadership in their respective political and religious spheres.

Secondly, the united kingdom of Saul's successors, David and Solomon, had split into Judah in the south with its centre at Jerusalem (on Mount Zion) and Israel in the north with its centres at Samaria, Bethel, Mount Carmel and Gilgal. These political changes were accompanied by religious changes and a few of the prophets, as they sought to interpret God's message for the time, found themselves in open opposition to the royal leadership and to its supporters (like Amaziah).

From the time of Amos there was a third factor at work. Over the horizon, beyond the borders of Judah and Israel, the nation of Assyria was growing in such strength that before long it would become a world power and threaten the safety of both Israel and Judah. See map (p. 64) and chart (inside back cover).

★ Amos was called by God to speak his word to Israel. God gave him a message that brought him into direct conflict with the leaders of the nations, and with other prophets such as Amaziah, because Amaziah was a prophetic spokesman *for* Israel whilst Amos spoke *against* that country, and *for* God.

Two prophets saw the same situation differently. We are going to further explore the insight that God gave to Amos using:

Find out how the prophet interprets the present situation

There are obviously two stages. One is to scour the text for factual information about the situation in Israel. The second is to see how God, through the prophet, interprets the situation. This is summarized in diagram 3 below.

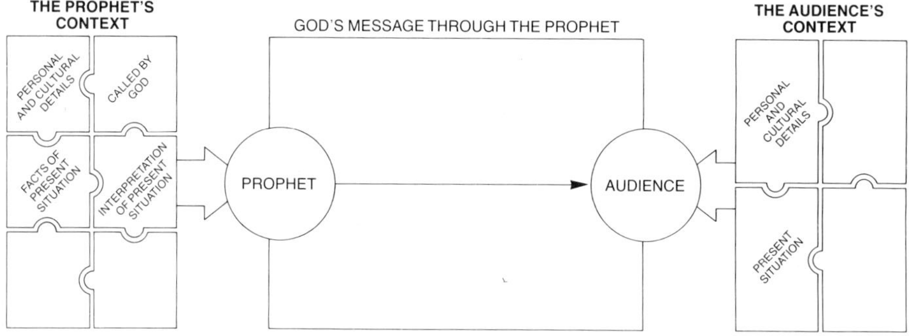

Diagram 3

★ Read the following passages.

---

4 Listen to this, you women of Samaria, who grow fat like the well-fed cows of Bashan, who ill-treat the weak, oppress the poor, and demand that your husbands keep you supplied with liquor! 2 As the Sovereign LORD is holy, he has promised, "The days will come when they will drag you away with hooks; every one of you will be like a fish on a hook. 3 You will be dragged to the nearest break in the wall and thrown out."

Israel's Failure to Learn

4 The Sovereign LORD says, "People of Israel, go to the holy place in Bethel and sin, if you must! Go to Gilgal and sin with all your might! Go ahead and bring animals to be sacrificed morning after morning, and bring your tithes every third day. 5 Go ahead and offer your bread in thanksgiving to God, and boast about the extra offerings you bring! This is the kind of thing you love to do.

6 "I was the one who brought famine to all your cities, yet you did not come back to me. 7 I held back the rain when your crops needed it most. I sent rain on one city, but not on another. Rain fell on one field, but another field dried up. 8 Weak with thirst, the people of several cities went to a city where they hoped to find water, but there was not enough to drink. Still you did not come back to me."

(Amos 4.1-8)

---

10 You people hate anyone who challenges injustice and speaks the whole truth in court. 11 You have oppressed the poor and robbed them of their grain. And so you will not live in the fine stone houses you build or drink wine from the beautiful vineyards you plant. 12 I know how terrible your sins are and how many crimes you have committed. You persecute good men, take bribes, and prevent the poor from getting justice in the courts. 13 And so, keeping quiet in such evil times is the clever thing to do!

14 Make it your aim to do what is right, not what is evil, so that you may live. Then the LORD God Almighty really will be with you, as you claim he is. 15 Hate what is evil, love what is right, and see that justice prevails in the courts. Perhaps the LORD will be merciful to the people of this nation who are still left alive.

16 And so the Sovereign LORD Almighty says, "There will be wailing and cries of sorrow in the city streets. Even farmers will be called to mourn the dead along with those who are paid to mourn. 17 There will be wailing in all the vineyards. All this will take place because I am coming to punish you." The LORD has spoken.

(Amos 5.10-17)

---

21 The LORD says, "I hate your religious festivals; I cannot stand them! 22 When you bring me burnt-offerings and grain-offerings, I will not accept them; I will not accept the animals you have fattened to bring me as offerings. 23 Stop your noisy songs; I do not want to listen to your harps. 24 Instead, let justice flow like a stream, and righteousness like a river that never goes dry."

(Amos 5.21-24)

★ Factual information

Split into three groups. Choose one of the headings below and gather all the information you can from the above passages about the state of the nation. At this stage try to record factual information rather than prophetic comment.

Group 1 – The political regime operating and its social life

. . . .

. . . .

. . . .

. . . .

Group 2 – The economic state of the country

. . . .

. . . .

. . . .

. . . .

Group 3 – The religious life of the nation

. . . .

. . . .

. . . .

. . . .

★ Share your findings, and note the observations made by the other groups.

Are there any parallels today?

★ Interpretation

The prophet's gift was not simply that of intellectual analysis – indeed, as God spoke to some prophets they were themselves confused by the message they had to pass on. It was beyond them. We shall look further at this fact in session 7. The word "interpretation" must be correctly understood. God is interpreting the situation through the prophet.

The whole group should now together examine the prophet's reaction to the situation.

How does God, through the prophet, interpret the situation described above? Note comments below.

Which of these factors strikes you as the most important?

Why was Amos in conflict with the nation's leaders?

★ Now summarize Amos' message. Look for any summary statements in the passage.

Message

. . . .

. . . .

. . . .

How do you feel about that message?

Application

★ The next exercise is an important preparation for some of the later sessions. You will have to refer back to it many times. So ensure that you have plenty of time (at least 20 minutes) to do this part.

For five minutes only, brainstorm – i.e., list but do not discuss – what you think are the important political, social and economic issues that face our own nation today. One person in the group write the suggestions on a large sheet of paper.

★ Now, on your own, make a quick list here of those you consider *most* important, adding any new ones you think of, if necessary.

Issue 1 ....

Issue 2 ....

Issue 3 ....

Issue 4 ....

Issue 5 ....

★ Discuss your list with the whole group and compile an agreed list of key issues in order of priority.

The group's list of key issues

Issue 1 ....

Issue 2 ....

Issue 3 ....

Issue 4 ....

On your own

A similar prophecy, though of a much later period, can be found in Haggai 1.

Summary of the third step

Find out how the prophet interprets the present situation

The past tradition

Aim
To see how history and tradition influenced a prophet's message.

Bible study

★ Seeing the prophets in context means seeing them under the influence of past tradition.
We begin this session by comparing the prophets Amos and Hosea, and their very different traditions.

★ Read the following passages:

---

1 This is the message which the LORD gave Hosea son of Beeri during the time that Uzziah, Jotham, Ahaz, and Hezekiah were kings of Judah, and Jeroboam son of Jehoash was king of Israel.

(Hosea 1.1)

God's Love for His Rebellious People

11 The LORD says,
"When Israel was a child, I loved him
and called him out of Egypt as my son.
2 But the more I called to him,
the more he turned away from me.
My people sacrificed to Baal;
they burnt incense to idols.
3 Yet I was the one who taught Israel to walk.
I took my people up in my arms,
but they did not acknowledge that I took care of them.
4 I drew them to me with affection and love.
I picked them up and held them to my cheek;
I bent down to them and fed them.

5 "They refuse to return to me, and so
they must return to Egypt, and Assyria
will rule them. 6 War will sweep through
their cities and break down the city gates.
It will destroy my people because they
do what they themselves think best. 7 They
insist on turning away from me. They will
cry out because of the yoke that is on
them, but no one will lift it from them.

8 "How can I give you up, Israel?
How can I abandon you?
Could I ever destroy you as I did Admah,
or treat you as I did Zeboiim?
My heart will not let me do it!
My love for you is too strong.
9 I will not punish you in my anger;
I will not destroy Israel again.
For I am God and not man.
I, the Holy One, am with you.
I will not come to you in anger.

10 "My people will follow me when I
roar like a lion at their enemies. They
will hurry to me from the west. 11 They
will come from Egypt, as swiftly as birds,
and from Assyria, like doves. I will bring
them to their homes again. I, the LORD,
have spoken."

(Hosea 11.1-11)

Background

Both Amos and Hosea preached in the northern kingdom of Israel in the middle of the eighth century. Hosea began his ministry after Amos had returned home to Judah. The Assyrian crisis was almost upon them, the invasion of Israel had begun. Soon the capital city of Samaria would be ransacked and its national life devastated.

★ Now refer back to session 3 and reread Amos 1.1-2 and Amos 4.1-8. On your own, note below the tone and content of each prophet's message.

Amos	Hosea
Emotional tone of message	
Content of message	

Then discuss this question as a whole group.

What do you think are the essential differences between Amos and Hosea?

★ In the last session we explored the great Old Testament prophets' interpretation of contemporary events. Because they were able to see the significance of events around them and compare these with other events at other times, they detected a golden thread running through history. There was purpose; history had meaning. Now for us today there is nothing new about this idea, but in the eighth and ninth centuries BC this was an important discovery. The modern dynamic view of history which characterizes western industrialized society springs from this Jewish prophetic tradition. Not that it always helps us to learn from our mistakes!

The prophet, however, was an inheritor and guardian of tradition. His knowledge of God's dealings with his own people gave him reason both for judgement and for hope. So:

Find out all you can about past tradition and its influence upon the prophet

★ Hosea, unlike Amos who came from Judah, spoke to Israel from within, as an Israelite, and shared the same common past.

Half the group reread the Hosea passages above, and the other half read the further passages below. Try to spot the ingredients of the tradition from which Hosea drew. Underline words or phrases which refer to religious events in the past, then discuss together how these have influenced the prophet's message in the present.

---

12 1 Everything that the people of
Israel do from morning to night
is useless and destructive. Treachery and
acts of violence increase among them.
They make treaties with Assyria and do
business with Egypt."
2 The LORD has an accusation to bring
against the people of Judah; he is also
going to punish Israel for the way her
people act. He will pay them back for
what they have done. 3 Their ancestor
Jacob struggled with his twin brother
Esau while the two of them were still in
their mother's womb; when Jacob grew
up, he fought against God—4 he fought
against an angel and won. He wept and
asked for a blessing. And at Bethel God
came to our ancestor Jacob and spoke
with him.[f] 5 This was the LORD God
Almighty—the LORD is the name by which
he is to be worshipped. 6 So now, descendants of Jacob, trust in your God and return
to him. Be loyal and just, and wait
patiently for your God to act.

Further Words of Judgement

7 The LORD says, "The people of Israel
are as dishonest as the Canaanites; they
love to cheat their customers with false
scales. 8 'We are rich,' they say. 'We've
made a fortune. And no one can accuse
us of getting rich dishonestly.' 9 But I, the
LORD your God who led you out of Egypt,
I will make you live in tents again, as you
did when I came to you in the desert."

(Hosea 12.1-9)

★ Now, as you did for Amos, produce your own summary statement of Hosea's message.

Message

. . . .

. . . .

. . . .

. . . .

. . . .

. . . .

What do you see as the most important traditions which influence you?

Background

Hosea drew from a very primitive tradition which went back to the promise given to Jacob. It especially emphasized God's almighty act of bringing Israel out of captivity in Egypt. This tradition emphasized how under Moses, God led the people into the desert in order to establish a special relationship (Covenant) with them, and to give them the law. Israel was to be a pilgrim people called to live and move under law and promise.

There was, however, another tradition, one from which Isaiah drew much of his inspiration. This tradition went back to David and, reflecting a later settled period, emphasized God's promise to establish David's throne for ever. To the citizens of Jerusalem, having survived the Assyrian onslaught, this later tradition not only fired their imagination but led to the popular belief that David's city was indestructible and its inhabitants secure for ever.

Jeremiah, on the other hand, drew his inspiration from the older Exodus and Covenant tradition and therefore found himself in conflict with almost everyone in Jerusalem.

This step is represented in diagram 4 below. Note the two particular strands of tradition.

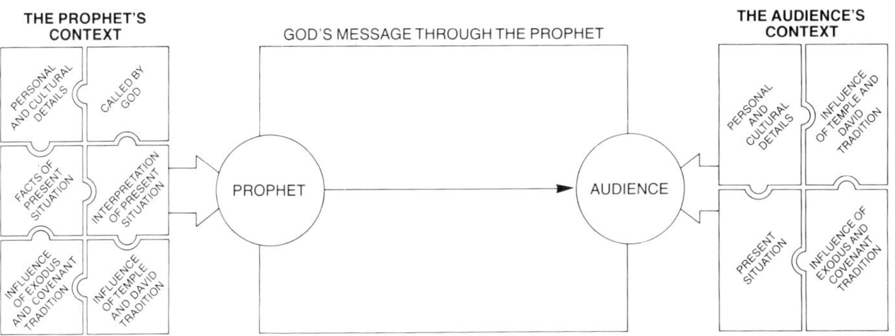

Diagram 4

What are the advantages and disadvantages of tradition?

Application

★ Divide into two groups, A and B. Take the first modern issue that was agreed in the last session, and prepare a prophetic comment on the issue. To prepare for this, which is a spiritual task, spend some minutes in prayer and meditation as a group. Ask the Holy Spirit to interpret and help you understand the situation.

Group A, do so from the perspective of Amos. Analyse the situation; adopt his tone; speak as an outsider and opponent.

Group B, prepare your comment from the perspective of Hosea. Your tone is one of anguished sympathy and pain; your argument should draw on traditions.

◔ Compare and discuss your "prophecies".

★ Finally, discuss together what you have learned from these first four sessions. If you intend to continue with Unit 2, then you should consider renewing your group promise or contract (see page 11) at this stage.

On your own

A similar perspective to that of Hosea is adopted in Jeremiah 2.

Summary of the fourth step

Find out all you can about past tradition and its influence upon the prophet

What God wants

Aim

To show how the rejection of a prophet's message led him to look to the future.

Bible study

★ In Unit 1, we concentrated on seeing the prophets in context. This context included their call by God, the present situation of the society in which they prophesied, and the past traditions which they inherited.

Unit 2 will concentrate on the prophet's message. What did the prophet have to say? How did he say it? What effect did it have?

Understanding the prophet's message means first of all understanding what God wanted of his people.

★ In the year 721 BC Samaria fell, and with it the northern kingdom of Israel. The message of doom pronounced by both Amos and Hosea (see previous two sessions) was thus confirmed by actual events. The tiny southern kingdom of Judah now lay exposed before the massive war machine of Assyria. The new imperial boundary ran only a few miles to the north of the capital, Jerusalem. The days of security and peace were over. A succession of kings, Jothan, Ahaz and Hezekiah sought to halt the advancing tide by building new defences, seeking foreign alliances, attempting to buy off the invader, and double-dealing in political deceit and intrigue. Only one man, Isaiah, clearly saw what was happening and prophesied against it.

Read the following passage which graphically portrays the scene and then consider the questions that follow it.

---

1 This book contains the messages
about Judah and Jerusalem which
God revealed to Isaiah son of Amoz during
the time when Uzziah, Jotham, Ahaz, and
Hezekiah were kings of Judah.

God Reprimands His People

2 The LORD said, "Earth and sky, listen
to what I am saying! The children I
brought up have rebelled against me.
3 Cattle know who owns them, and don-
keys know where their master feeds them.
But that is more than my people Israel
know. They don't understand at all."

4 You are doomed, you sinful nation,
you corrupt and evil people! Your sins
drag you down! You have rejected the
LORD, the holy God of Israel, and have
turned your backs on him. 5 Why do you
keep on rebelling? Do you want to be
punished even more? Israel, your head
is already covered with wounds, and your
heart and mind are sick. 6 From head to
foot there is not a healthy spot on your
body. You are covered with bruises and
sores and open wounds. Your wounds
have not been cleaned or bandaged. No
ointment has been put on them.

7 Your country has been devastated,

and your cities have been burnt to the
ground. While you look on, foreigners
take over your land and bring everything
to ruin. 8 Jerusalem alone is left, a city
under siege—as defenceless as a watch-
man's hut in a vineyard or a shed in a
cucumber field. 9 If the LORD Almighty had
not let some of the people survive,
Jerusalem would have been totally destroyed, just as Sodom and Gomorrah
were.

10 Jerusalem, your rulers and your
people are like those of Sodom and
Gomorrah. Listen to what the LORD is
saying to you. Pay attention to what our
God is teaching you. 11 He says, "Do you
think I want all these sacrifices you keep
offering to me? I have had more than
enough of the sheep you burn as sacrifices
and of the fat of your fine animals. I am
tired of the blood of bulls and sheep and
goats. 12 Who asked you to bring me all
this when you come to worship me? Who
asked you to do all this tramping about
in my Temple? 13 It's useless to bring your
offerings. I am disgusted with the smell
of the incense you burn. I cannot stand
your New Moon Festivals, your Sabbaths,
and your religious gatherings; they are
all corrupted by your sins. 14 I hate your
New Moon Festivals and holy days; they
are a burden that I am tired of bearing.

15 "When you lift your hands in prayer,
I will not look at you. No matter how
much you pray, I will not listen, for your
hands are covered with blood. 16 Wash
yourselves clean. Stop all this evil that
I see you doing. Yes, stop doing evil 17 and
learn to do right. See that justice is done—
help those who are oppressed, give
orphans their rights, and defend widows."

18 The LORD says, "Now, let's settle the
matter. You are stained red with sin, but
I will wash you as clean as snow.
Although your stains are deep red, you
will be as white as wool. 19 If you will
only obey me, you will eat the good things
the land produces. 20 But if you defy me,
you are doomed to die. I, the LORD, have
spoken."

(Isaiah 1.1–20)

Note: Israel in verse 3 refers to the southern kingdom of Judah.

What is the current situation in Judah?
Why is Isaiah's message rejected?
How does the prophet interpret this situation?
Why does God bother with Israel when they keep on sinning?

★ Against this background, Isaiah committed his words to writing as an act of judgement on the present generation and as a sign of hope for some future generation (see Isaiah 30.8-11 below).

The Disobedient People

8 God told me to write down in a book
what the people are like, so that there
would be a permanent record of how evil
they are. 9 They are always rebelling
against God, always lying, always re-
fusing to listen to the LORD's teachings.
10 They tell the prophets to keep quiet.
They say, "Don't talk to us about what's
right. Tell us what we want to hear. Let
us keep our illusions. 11 Get out of our way
and stop blocking our path. We don't want
to hear about your holy God of Israel."

(Isaiah 30.8-11)

★ In understanding the prophet's message it is vital to realize that God does not just *comment* on the situation of the world. He actively seeks to *change* it, by changing the hearts of men and women.

Through the prophet, God looks for a response. So:

Discover what response God requires in the face of the impending crisis

As with Step 3, this can be seen in two parts. One, "What does God say is going to happen in the future?" and two, "What does God want the people to do now?"

This is represented in diagram 5 below.

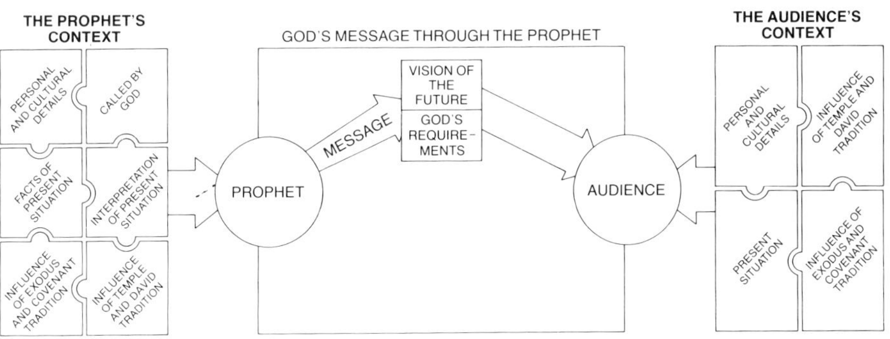

Diagram 5

★ What does God say is going to happen?

Read the following passages and identify the different forecasts for the future that Isaiah predicted. Summarize each one.

Background

Within a prophetic book, the various oracles and stories do not necessarily follow one another in a normal chronological order. Like the Bible itself, the various strands of material were gathered together over a period of time. Unlike modern editors, in Isaiah's time they were not greatly concerned about putting things in an historical order.

The Fate of Jerusalem

29 God's altar, Jerusalem itself, is
doomed! The city where David
camped is doomed! Let another year or
two come and go, with its feasts and
festivals, 2 and then God will bring disaster
on the city that is called "God's altar."
There will be weeping and wailing, and the
whole city will be like an altar covered
with blood. 3 God will attack the city,
surround it, and besiege it. 4 Jerusalem will
be like a ghost struggling to speak from
under the ground, a muffled voice coming
from the dust.
5 Jerusalem, all the foreigners who
attack you will be blown away like dust,
and their terrifying armies will fly away
like straw. Suddenly and unexpectedly
6 the LORD Almighty will rescue you with
violent thunderstorms and earthquakes.
He will send tempests and raging fire;
7 then all the armies of the nations
attacking the city of God's altar, all their
weapons and equipment—everything—
will vanish like a dream, like something
imagined in the night. 8 All the nations
that assemble to attack Jerusalem will be
like a starving man who dreams he is
eating and wakes up hungry, or like a
man dying of thirst who dreams he is
drinking and wakes with a dry throat.

(Isaiah 29.1-8)

Summary ....

....

....

....

....

....

The Exiled People Will Return

10 A day is coming when the new king
from the royal line of David will be a
symbol to the nations. They will gather
in his royal city and give him honour.

11 When that day comes, the Lord will
once again use his power and bring back
home those of his people who are left
in Assyria and Egypt, in the lands of
Pathros, Sudan, Elam, Babylonia, and
Hamath, and in the coastlands and on
the islands of the sea. 12 The LORD will
raise a signal flag to show the nations
that he is gathering together again the
scattered people of Israel and Judah and
bringing them back from the four corners
of the earth.

(Isaiah 11.10-12)

Summary ....

....

....

....

....

....

The LORD Will Punish Assyria

24 The Sovereign LORD Almighty says
to his people who live in Zion, "Do not
be afraid of the Assyrians, even though
they oppress you as the Egyptians used
to do. 25 In only a little while I will finish
punishing you, and then I will destroy
them. 26 I, the LORD Almighty, will beat
them with my whip as I beat the people
of Midian at the Rock of Oreb. I will
punish Assyria as I punished Egypt.
27 When that time comes, I will free you
from the power of Assyria, and their yoke
will no longer be a burden on your
shoulders."

(Isaiah 10.24-27)

Summary ....

....

....

....

....

....

How do we reconcile some of the conflicting prophecies?

★ **What does God want the people to do?**
Look again at the four passages from Isaiah used in this session and identify what actions or attitudes God wants the people to adopt. Underline anything which seems important, and share them with the rest of the group.

★ Now summarize Isaiah's message, as you understand it so far.

Message

....

....

....

....

....

....

....

Discuss together as a group:

What can we learn from Isaiah's message?

Application

★ In the last session you made a "prophetic comment" in the style of Hosea and Amos. This next activity allows both your experience of the other prophets *and* your own judgements to combine in prophetic activity.

★ Remind yourself of the "issues" you listed on page 30 (session 3).
Choose as many of the issues as you wish. Split into sub-groups – one to work on each issue. In these sub-groups consider:

Which of the prophets so far studied seems the most relevant to this issue?

If the situation remains as now – with nothing changing for the better – what might happen?

What do you think God wants *you* to do about it?

What do you think God wants *others* to do about it?

★ Having discussed this final question, define as clearly as possible the audience with whom you would like to share this message. We will return to this next week. For the time being, complete the table below to focus your thoughts. Decide on the audience that you will be addressing. It must be a real audience and you must be familiar with the place where they gather. It could be a local congregation or a community group or crowds in a shopping precinct. Define exactly what you wish to say to alert this group to the issue and clearly indicate the response people should make as a result. Use this space to record your conclusions.

Audience ....

....

....

....

Meeting place ....

....

Issue chosen ....

....

....

....

....

....

....

N.B. If you run out of time you can continue this exercise at the next session.

For next time

We shall be doing some drama, so we need space and "props". The leader should read through the next session and get suitable "props" together.

On your own

Micah, a contemporary of Isaiah, also lived in the southern kingdom of Judah, but unlike his more illustrious and high ranking companion who had the ear of kings and princes, Micah moved in humble circles and ministered in a small country town. Though the two never met, as far as we know, Micah's message is very similar. Read chapters 3 and 4 of Micah and compare it with Isaiah's message explored in this session.

Summary of the fifth step

Discover what response God requires in the face of the impending crisis

How to communicate it

Aim
To examine the methods the prophets used to get people to understand and respond.

Bible study

★ Understanding the prophet's message requires understanding the methods the prophet used to get it across.

★ Read through the passages below. Look again at the summary statements you have made about the message of the prophets Isaiah (page 42) and Hosea (page 34). In the light of this information, discuss:

What do you think their actions in the following passages are supposed to mean?
Can you spot any differences in style? Are they typical of that prophet?

For Isaiah

2Three years earlier the LORD had told
Isaiah son of Amoz to take off his sandals
and the sackcloth he was wearing. He
obeyed and went about naked and barefoot. 3When Ashdod was captured, the
LORD said, "My servant Isaiah has been
going about naked and barefoot for three
years. This is a sign of what will happen
to Egypt and Sudan."

(Isaiah 20.2-3)

For Hosea

Hosea's Wife and Children

2 When the LORD first spoke to Israel
through Hosea, he said to Hosea, "Go and
get married; your wife will be unfaithful,
and your children will be just like her.
In the same way, my people have left
me and become unfaithful."
3 So Hosea married a woman named
Gomer, the daughter of Diblaim. After the
birth of their first child, a son, 4the LORD
said to Hosea, "Name him 'Jezreel,'
because it will not be long before I punish
the king of Israel for the murders that
his ancestor Jehu committed at Jezreel.
I am going to put an end to Jehu's
dynasty."

(Hosea 1.2-4)

★ In their desire to communicate the message God had given them the prophets did not limit themselves to words alone. They knew that their

God was not only one who gave them revelations, he was a God who did things. If they were to be true to him then the prophetic message had to be communicated by deeds and signs as well as words. So:

Examine the method of communication used by the prophet

This is set out in diagram 6 below.

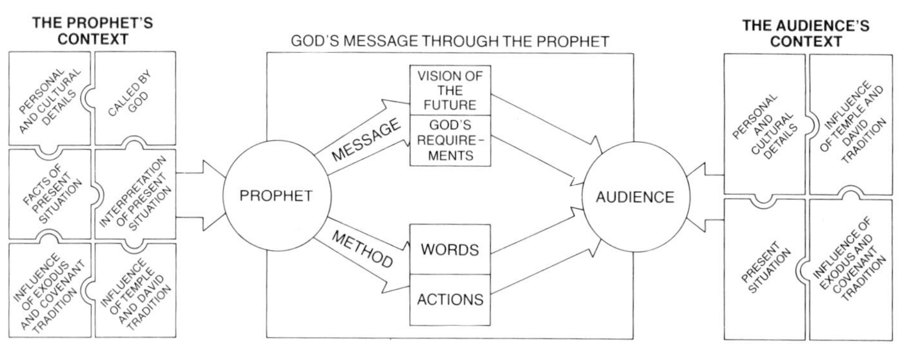

Diagram 6

★ Read the background below concerning the prophet Ezekiel before going on to explore his methods of communication.

Background

In 598 BC Nebuchadnezzer attacked and ransacked Jerusalem (see chart on inside back cover). He stole the Temple treasures and deported King Jehoiachim and all the leading officials back to Babylon, after appointing Zedekiah as his puppet king. Jeremiah was left behind but another prophet, Ezekiel, was carried off with the exiles. As a member of Jerusalem's priestly upper class, he continued to exercise a strong influence upon his fellow-countrymen.

Like the other exiles, he experienced grief and shock at what had happened and again and again he returned in spirit to his beloved city and temple. His book is filled with symbols and pictures, a dream language which drew on knowledge of both priestly rites in the Temple and pagan imagery in Babylon.

More importantly, in him some of the key features of both Isaiah and Jeremiah came together. He combined, for the first time, the Exodus and Jerusalem traditions, and his call reflected both Isaiah's stirring vision and Jeremiah's verbal inspiration.

★ As part of our attempt to understand the prophet's message we are going to explore the methods of communication used by the prophet.

Split into two Groups, A and B. Pick one passage each from the two passages below and from it produce a dramatic presentation. They require two very different pieces of drama.

The first passage is almost scripted for drama already. The action is humorous. Ask yourselves: where is Ezekiel when he gets this instruction? How does he react to it? How do others react to him? When he has finished the action, how does he convey to *his* audience the meaning of this dramatic parable? How can you convey that meaning to your audience?

Use words very sparingly. If possible limit yourselves only to the words of the Bible passage.

The second passage cannot be presented so literally, but as a poem, with strong images, it can be translated into an effective piece of drama. Ask yourselves, What is the mood of the "poem"?

How can that mood best be conveyed – as a song? a lullaby? What are the main images? Can they be presented dramatically? How does Ezekiel convey his meaning to his audience? How can you convey that meaning to yours?

Make use of the "props" provided if you need them. Your task is to present the passage in such a dramatic way that an audience is provoked to question and respond. You have 20 minutes to prepare your presentation.

Ezekiel Cuts His Hair

5 The LORD said, "Mortal man, take a
sharp sword and use it to shave off
your beard and all your hair. Then weigh
the hair on scales and divide it into three
parts. 2 Burn a third of it in the city when

the siege is over. Take another third and
chop it up with your sword as you move
about outside the city. Scatter the remain-
ing third to the winds, and I will pursue
it with my sword. 3 Keep back a few hairs
and wrap them in the hem of your clothes.
4 Then take a few of them out again, throw
them in the fire, and let them burn up.
From them fire will spread to the whole
nation of Israel."
11 "Therefore, as I am the living God—
this is the word of the Sovereign LORD—
because you defiled my Temple with all
the evil, disgusting things you did, I will
cut you down without mercy. 12 A third
of your people will die from sickness and
hunger in the city; a third will be cut
down by swords outside the city; and I
will scatter the last third to the winds
and pursue them with a sword."

(Ezekiel 5.1-4, 11-12)

Egypt Is Compared to a Cedar Tree

31 On the first day of the third month
of the eleventh year of our exile,
the LORD spoke to me. 2 "Mortal man,"
he said, "say to the king of Egypt and
all his people:

How powerful you are!
What can I compare you to?
3 You are like a cedar in Lebanon,
With beautiful, shady branches,
A tree so tall it reaches the clouds.
4 There was water to make it grow,
And underground rivers to feed it.
They watered the place where the tree was growing
And sent streams to all the trees of the forest.
5 Because it was well-watered,
It grew taller than other trees.
Its branches grew thick and long.
6 Every kind of bird built nests in its branches;
The wild animals bore their young in its shelter;
The nations of the world rested in its shade.
7 How beautiful the tree was—
So tall, with such long branches.
Its roots reached down to the deep-flowing streams.
8 No cedar in God's garden could compare with it.
No fir-tree ever had such branches,
And no plane-tree such boughs.
No tree in God's own garden was so beautiful.
9 I made it beautiful, with spreading branches.
It was the envy of every tree in Eden, the garden of God.

10 "Now then, I, the Sovereign LORD,
will tell you what is going to happen to
that tree that grew until it reached the
clouds. As it grew taller it grew proud;
11 so I have rejected it and will let a foreign
ruler have it. He will give that tree what
it deserves for its wickedness. 12 Ruthless
foreigners will cut it down and leave it.
Its branches and broken boughs will fall
on every mountain and valley in the
country. All the nations that have been
living in its shade will go away. 13 The
birds will come and perch on the fallen
tree, and the wild animals will walk over
its branches."

(Ezekiel 31.1-13)

★ Each group should present its piece of drama to the other group. Comment on them and discuss how well they succeeded in conveying the prophet's message. Then discuss:

Are there parallels to how people seek to communicate their message today?

Do you think there are disadvantages to communicating in this way?

Application

★ Refer back to the message and audience you defined in session 5 (page 43). Create a dramatic presentation (as did Ezekiel) which will hammer home the issue and evoke the required response. Decide when you are going to perform this. Fix a date and a time and perform it, if possible, ◑ before the next session as we will want to reflect on the experience.

For next time

We shall need space again for a role-play, though no props.

On your own

Two further passages which you can meditate on and indeed act out, are Ezekiel 24.15-19 and Ezekiel 37.1-10.

Summary of the sixth step

Examine the method of communication used by the prophet

Living it out

Aim

To see how the prophet himself was affected by the message he received.

Bible study

★ Understanding the prophet's message requires understanding its effect on the prophet himself.

In our study of Isaiah we saw that his regard for the future led him, when his words were rejected, to write them down and thus preserve them for a later generation. As time goes on we find that words are written down not only by the prophet but also by a small circle of his disciples who themselves have come to recognize the truth of what has been said.

Our study of Ezekiel highlighted a further feature. Prophets used every means possible to communicate, and in doing so the prophet himself became a visible sign of the message given to him. Thus a prophet's disciples found themselves not only recording the message but engaging in an almost modern biographical exercise. This reaches a peak in the book of Jeremiah with its mixture of preaching and biography faithfully recorded by Jeremiah's secretary, Baruch. Such accounts give us a fascinating insight into the personal life of the prophet, as well as helping us to understand and apply the prophecy today. So:

Identify with the emotional condition of the prophet

★ We are going to begin with an exercise to help us relate to the feelings and emotions of people in a story from the life of Jeremiah.

Try to discover the view-points, arguments and feelings of the people in the following passages.

Form two groups, A and B, to examine the passages below. Group A should concentrate on Elishama and the court officials "who showed no sign of sorrow" (verse 24).

Group B should concentrate on Baruch, Elnathan, Delaiah etc.

Try to feel what they feel. Try to identify with them. Consider the following questions:

Why do your characters do what they do?
How do they feel about the other characters?

Baruch Reads the Scroll in the Temple

36 In the fourth year that Jehoiakim
son of Josiah was king of Judah,
the LORD said to me, 2 "Get a scroll and
write on it everything that I have told
you about Israel and Judah and all the
nations. Write everything that I have told
you from the time I first spoke to you,
when Josiah was king, up to the present.
3 Perhaps when the people of Judah hear
about all the destruction that I intend to
bring on them, they will turn from their
evil ways. Then I will forgive their
wickedness and their sins."
4 So I called Baruch son of Neriah and
dictated to him everything that the LORD
had said to me. And Baruch wrote it all
down on a scroll. 5 Then I gave Baruch
the following instructions: "I am no
longer allowed to go into the Temple. 6 But
I want you to go there the next time the
people are fasting. You are to read the
scroll aloud, so that they will hear
everything that the LORD has said to me
and that I have dictated to you. Do this
where everyone can hear you, including
the people of Judah who have come in
from their towns. 7 Perhaps they will pray
to the LORD and turn from their evil ways,
because the LORD has threatened this
people with his terrible anger and fury."
8 So Baruch read the LORD's words in the
Temple exactly as I had told him to do.

(Jeremiah 36.1-8)

---

14 Then the officials sent Jehudi
(the son of Nethaniah, grandson of
Shelemiah, and great-grandson of Cushi)
to tell Baruch to bring the scroll that he
had read to the people. Baruch brought
them the scroll. 15 "Sit down," they said,
"and read the scroll to us." So Baruch
did. 16 After he had read it, they turned
to one another in alarm, and said to
Baruch, "We must report this to the king."
17 Then they asked him, "Tell us, now, how
did you come to write all this? Did
Jeremiah dictate it to you?"
18 Baruch answered, "Jeremiah dictated every word of it to me, and I wrote
it down in ink on this scroll."
19 Then they said to him, "You and
Jeremiah must go and hide. Don't let
anyone know where you are."

The King Burns the Scroll

20 The officials put the scroll in the
room of Elishama, the court secretary, and
went to the king's court, where they
reported everything to the king. 21 Then
the king sent Jehudi to get the scroll. He
took it from the room of Elishama and
read it to the king and all the officials who
were standing round him. 22 It was winter
and the king was sitting in his winter
palace in front of the fire. 23 As soon as
Jehudi finished reading three or four
columns, the king cut them off with a
small knife and threw them into the fire.
He kept doing this until the entire scroll
was burnt up. 24 But neither the king nor
any of his officials who heard all this was
afraid or showed any sign of sorrow.
25 Although Elnathan, Delaiah, and
Gemariah begged the king not to burn
the scroll, he paid no attention to them.
26 Then he ordered Prince Jerahmeel,
together with Seraiah son of Azriel and
Shelemiah son of Abdeel, to arrest me
and my secretary Baruch. But the LORD
had hidden us.

Jeremiah Writes Another Scroll

27 After King Jehoiakim had burnt the
scroll that I had dictated to Baruch, the
LORD told me 28 to take another scroll and
write on it everything that had been on
the first one. 29 The LORD told me to say
to the king, "You have burnt the scroll,
and you have asked Jeremiah why he
wrote that the king of Babylonia would

come and destroy this land and kill its
people and its animals. 30 So now, I, the
LORD, say to you, King Jehoiakim, that
no descendant of yours will ever rule over
David's kingdom. Your corpse will be
thrown out where it will be exposed to
the sun during the day and to the frost
at night. 31 I will punish you, your descendants, and your officials because of the
sins all of you commit. Neither you nor
the people of Jerusalem and of Judah have
paid any attention to my warnings, and
so I will bring on all of you the disaster
that I have threatened."
32 Then I took another scroll and gave
it to my secretary Baruch, and he wrote
down everything that I dictated. He wrote
everything that had been on the first scroll
and similar messages that I dictated to
him.

(Jeremiah 36.14-32)

★ After 10 minutes get back together. Volunteers should role-play, i.e., spontaneously act out the story, expressing the characters' feelings about Jeremiah and his prophecy.

Use your own words. Tell the king what you think ought to happen to Jeremiah. You need one representative for each group and someone to play the king.

★ Having watched these role-plays, working as one group, think yourselves into Jeremiah's feelings. Try to get inside him and feel what he feels. What has happened to him physically? What has happened to him mentally and spiritually? Discuss:

What kind of person was Jeremiah?
How would he have been received in our own society?

★ Now, on your own, *assuming that you are Jeremiah*, describe your own feelings in words. Record those words below.

★ In addition to the biography recorded by Baruch, we also have an autobiography – a record of the prophet's deepest feelings and experiences. We shall be looking at those next. Diagram 7 below shows these new elements and the way in which the prophets' disciples built them into the prophetic tradition.

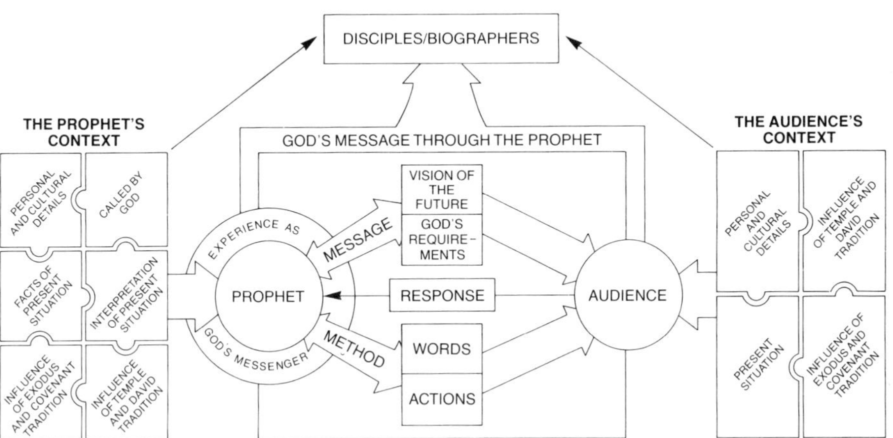

Diagram 7

The "confessions" of Jeremiah are scattered throughout the book. They provide windows into his soul.

Look at the passages below which reveal the prophet's mental pain, and compare them with the statements you have written. Discuss them as a group.

Jeremiah's Sorrow for His People

19 The pain! I can't bear the pain!
My heart! My heart is beating wildly!
I can't keep quiet;
I hear the trumpets
and the shouts of battle.

Jeremiah 4.19

21 My heart has been crushed
because my people are crushed;
I mourn; I am completely dismayed.
22 Is there no medicine in Gilead?
9 I wish my head were a well of water,
and my eyes a fountain of tears,
so that I could cry day and night
for my people who have been killed.
2 I wish I had a place to stay in the desert
where I could get away from my
people.
They are all unfaithful,
a mob of traitors.

(Jeremiah 8.21-9.2)

---

15 Then I said, "LORD, you understand.
Remember me and help me. Let me have
revenge on those who persecute me. Do
not be so patient with them that they
succeed in killing me. Remember that it
is for your sake that I am insulted. 16 You
spoke to me, and I listened to every word.
I belong to you, LORD God Almighty, and
so your words filled my heart with joy
and happiness. 17 I did not spend my time
with other people, laughing and having
a good time. In obedience to your orders
I stayed by myself and was filled with
anger. 18 Why do I keep on suffering? Why
are my wounds incurable? Why won't
they heal? Do you intend to disappoint
me like a stream that goes dry in the
summer?"

(Jeremiah 15.15-18)

Jeremiah Complains to the LORD

7 LORD, you have deceived me,
and I was deceived.
You are stronger than I am,
and you have overpowered me.
Everyone jeers at me;
they mock me all day long.

8 Whenever I speak, I have to cry out
and shout, "Violence! Destruction!"
LORD, I am ridiculed and scorned all
the time
because I proclaim your message.

(Jeremiah 20.7 8)

---

18 Why was I born?
Was it only to have trouble and
sorrow,
to end my life in disgrace?

(Jeremiah 20.18)

Why do you think it is so painful to be God's messenger?

★ Finally, summarize Jeremiah's message.

Message

. . . .

. . . .

. . . .

. . . .

. . . .

. . . .

Application

★ Reflect on the presentation you made in the intervening week. How did it go? What did you feel? What was the response of the audience?

Does your experience parallel those of the prophets we have examined?

What did you learn from the experience?

Consider your own feelings, for example:

Do you fear being laughed at for your beliefs or do you enjoy being different?

To what extent do these feelings influence the things you attempt to do for God?

On your own

In a very different way, the book of Jonah illustrates the experience of being God's messenger. See chapters 3 and 4.

Summary of the seventh step

Identify with the emotional condition of the prophet

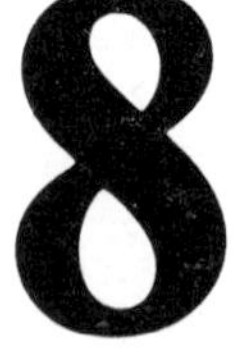

How is prophecy fulfilled?

Aim
To see how prophecies are fulfilled.

Bible study

★ Understanding a prophet's message requires understanding the different ways this message may be fulfilled. We begin with some background material that relates to Isaiah's prophecies studied in session 5.

Background

In 538 BC Cyrus issued an edict which allowed the Jews to go back home to Jerusalem. Isaiah's prophecies were fulfilled. There was, however, no glorious exodus of celebrating pilgrims; no sudden ecological transformation. The return was much more modest, little more than a trickle of groups over a period of years.

They found their beloved city in ruins. Refugees of many nations dwelt in hovels and scratched out an existence in the rubble. Soon the early enthusiasm of the exiles waned. There were difficulties in maintaining the re-established religious practices. Isaiah 55-56 reflects this period. Ambitious plans to rebuild the Temple were postponed until the prophet Haggai challenged the people.

There were resettlement problems, economic hardships, and clashes with the unsympathetic neigbours. Even when the Temple was rebuilt, it lacked splendour. Resources were scarce. These were not years of greatness, but of survival and this is reflected in the prophets of the time such as Zechariah. The vision was now clouded and the sound was muted. Morale and faith were kept alive by reiterating past conviction and by giving people "dreams" of a future. One hundred years later even those voices were silent. God would have to look for other ways of communicating his message.

★ Read the passage below.

The Prophet's Vision of the Horses

7 In the second year that Darius was
emperor, on the twenty-fourth day of the
eleventh month (the month of Shebat),
the LORD gave me a message in a vision
at night. 8 I saw an angel of the LORD
riding a red horse. He had stopped among
some myrtle-trees in a valley, and behind
him were other horses—red, dappled, and
white. 9 I asked him, "Sir, what do these
horses mean?"
He answered, "I will show you what
they mean. 10 The LORD sent them to go
and inspect the earth."
11 They reported to the angel: "We
have been all over the world and have
found that the whole world lies helpless
and subdued."
12 Then the angel said, "Almighty LORD,
you have been angry with Jerusalem and
the cities of Judah for seventy years now.
How much longer will it be before you
show them mercy?"
13 The LORD answered the angel with
comforting words, 14 and the angel told
me to proclaim what the LORD Almighty
had said: "I have a deep love and concern
for Jerusalem, my holy city, 15 and I am
very angry with the nations that enjoy
quiet and peace. For while I was holding
back my anger against my people, those
nations made the sufferings of my people
worse. 16 So I have come back to Jerusalem to show mercy to the city. My
Temple will be restored, and the city will
be rebuilt."
17 The angel also told me to proclaim:
"The LORD Almighty says that his cities
will be prosperous again and that he will
once again help Jerusalem and claim the
city as his own."

The Vision of the Horns

18 In another vision I saw four ox horns.
19 I asked the angel that had been speaking
to me, "What do these horns mean?"
He answered, "They stand for the world
powers that have scattered the people of
Judah, Israel, and Jerusalem."
20 Then the LORD showed me four
workmen with hammers. 21 I asked,
"What have these men come to do?"
He answered, "They have come to
terrify and overthrow the nations that
completely crushed the land of Judah and
scattered its people."

(Zechariah 1.7-21)

★ Discuss the following questions together.

What is the meaning of the various images?
How does it fit in with the background material?
How does the passage compare with passages you have read in Isaiah and Jeremiah?

★ We have seen that the prophets drew on past tradition, spoke out against current trends, and looked increasingly to the future. They became travellers on God's road of exploration. They moved forward like history itself. All the time their understanding of God's plans became deeper. Only the coming of God himself into history could completely fulfil their hopes and dreams. So:

State in what sense a prophet's hopes have been fulfilled

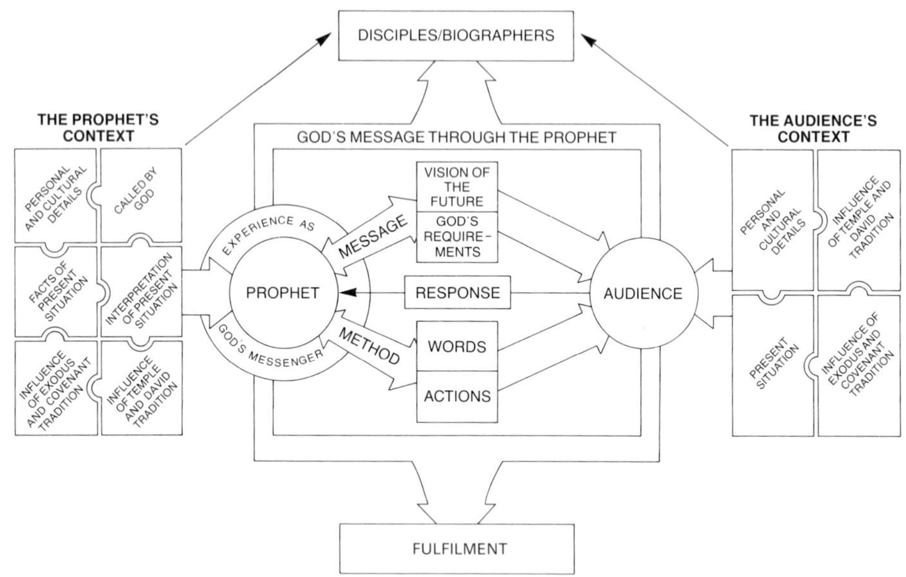

Diagram 8

★ Many of the things about which the prophets spoke did not take place in their own lifetime. This is only to be expected as God works on a larger time scale. Sometimes fulfillment came in a quite different way from that originally expected. For example, the return to and restoration of Jerusalem was a much more modest affair then Isaiah had described. Other prophetic hopes appear to be unfulfilled, but Christians believe that with the coming of Jesus many of these prophecies have come true.

★ Read the following passages and consider the following questions:

Has Jesus fulfilled this scripture in any way?
Has the Christian church fulfilled this scripture in any way?
Is there any sense in which it has not been fulfilled?

4 "But he endured the suffering that
should have been ours,
the pain that we should have borne.
All the while we thought that his
suffering
was punishment sent by God.
5 But because of our sins he was wounded,
beaten because of the evil we did.
We are healed by the punishment he
suffered,
made whole by the blows he received.
6 All of us were like sheep that were lost,
each of us going his own way.
But the LORD made the punishment fall
on him,
the punishment all of us deserved."

(Isaiah 53.4-6)

---

31 The LORD says, "The time is coming
when I will make a new covenant with
the people of Israel and with the people
of Judah. 32 It will not be like the old
covenant that I made with their ancestors
when I took them by the hand and led
them out of Egypt. Although I was like
a husband to them, they did not keep
that covenant. 33 The new covenant that
I will make with the people of Israel will
be this: I will put my law within them
and write it on their hearts. I will be their
God, and they will be my people. 34 None
of them will have to teach his fellow-countryman to know the LORD, because all will know me, from the least to the greatest. I will forgive their sins and I will no longer remember their wrongs. I, the LORD, have spoken."

(Jeremiah 31.31-34)

---

24 I will take you from every nation
and country and bring you back to your
own land. 25 I will sprinkle clean water
on you and make you clean from all your
idols and everything else that has defiled
you. 26 I will give you a new heart and
a new mind. I will take away your
stubborn heart of stone and give you an
obedient heart. 27 I will put my spirit in
you and I will see to it that you follow
my laws and keep all the commands I
have given you. 28 Then you will live in
the land I gave your ancestors. You will
be my people, and I will be your God.
29 I will save you from everything that
defiles you. I will command the corn to
be plentiful, so that you will not have
any more famines. 30 I will increase the
yield of your fruit-trees and your fields,
so that there will be no more famines
to disgrace you among the nations.

(Ezekiel 36.24-30)

Application

★ Turn back to session 1 and look at your definition of a prophet. In the light of this study, do you wish to change your definition?

My revised definition of a prophet is ....

....

....

....

....

....

★ Finally, consider the impact of *The Prophets* on you. Discuss these three questions together, as a group.

Has this course changed your perception of the Old Testament in any way?
Has it encouraged you to dig deeper into the Bible?
Is there any one prophet who has particularly captured your imagination? Who? Why?

Conclude with a discussion of what you wish to do next as a group. Maybe it means further dramatic presentations, but focusing on other issues and addressing new audiences.

Maybe, in a few months' time, you could use another *Jigsaw* book – *New Testament Letters* is an ideal next step, where the focus of interest is the "Church" rather than the "world".

Summary of the eighth step

State in what sense a prophet's hopes have been fulfilled

Conclusion

The Bible has infinite horizons which you can continue to explore, both in a group and on your own. May I encourage you to continue reading the Bible. Set yourself the task of reading through one of the major prophets who caught your imagination. Apply the insights you have learnt. Or maybe you should simply read through the smaller prophetic books. Read the Bible aloud, read it quietly to yourself. Above all, read it prayerfully in the expectation that through its pages you will hear the word of the living God.

Other books in this series
New Testament Letters
Gospels
Old Testament History
The Law
Poetry and Wisdom

One volume to cover each form of writing in the Bible. The whole series builds up into a valuable reference tool, and a stimulating approach to Bible study.

NOTES

NOTES

THE DIVIDED
ISRAELITE KINGDOMS
Sidon
ASSYRIA
Damascus
Mount Lebanon
Zarephath
SYRIA
Ijon
Abel Beth Maacah
Dan
NAPHTALI
BASHAN
Kedesh
GALILEE
Hazor
MEDITERRANEAN SEA
Aphek
River Kishon
Mount Carmel
Gath Hepher
LAKE GALILEE
EAST
MANASSEH
Megiddo
Shunem
Jezreel
Ramoth in Gilead
Dothan
Beth Shan
Tishbe
ISRAEL
Brook of Cherith
GILEAD
Samaria
Tirzah
GAD
AMMON
Shechem
River Jordan
Penuel
Tappuah
Shiloh
EPHRAIM
Bethel
Gilgal
Gezer
Ramah
Gibbethon
Anathoth
Ekron
BENJAMIN
Beth Shemesh
Jerusalem
REUBEN
Libnah
PHILISTIA
JUDAH
Gath
Lachish
Gaza
DEAD SEA
Aroer
JUDAH
River Arnon
MOAB
Beersheba
MOAB
0
20
40
60
Kilometres
EDOM